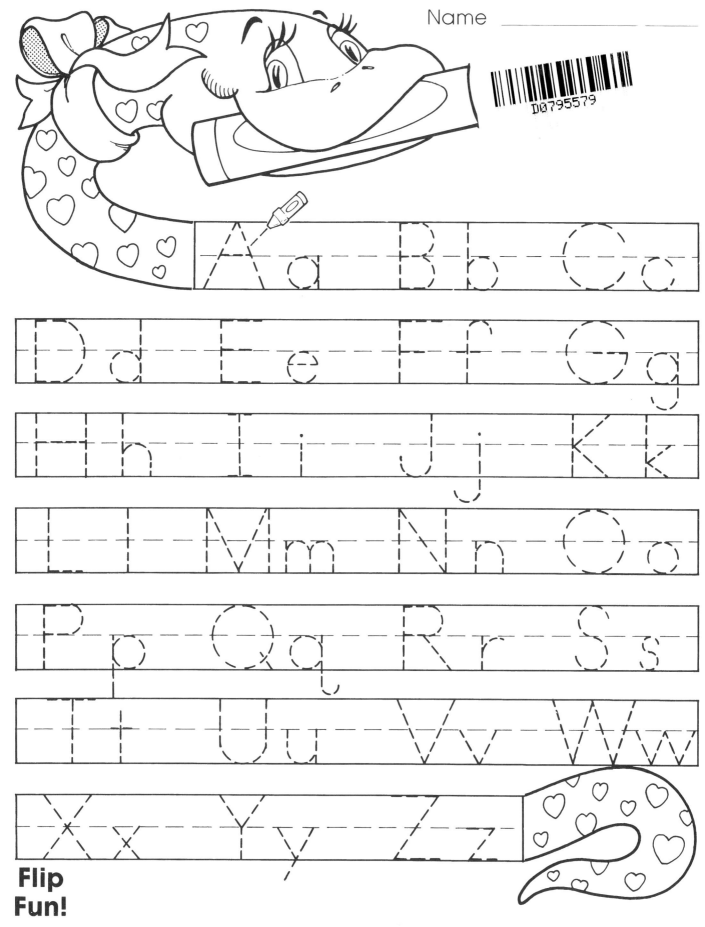

Name _____

Aa Bb Cc

Dd Ee Ff Gg

Hh Ii Jj Kk

Ll Mm Nn Oo

Pp Qq Rr Ss

Tt Uu Vv Ww

Xx Yy Zz

Flip Fun!

Draw an animal that begins with A and an animal that begins with Z.

3   0-88012-825-9 • Traditional Manuscript

A a

A A A A A A

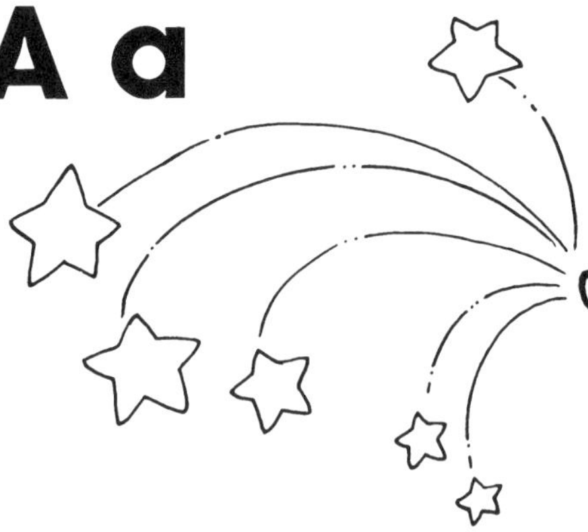

a a a a a a

A A

a a

A a A a

alligator

Alaska

**Flip
Fun!**

Draw three things that begin with A.

Name _____

Flip Fun!

Choose your favorite letter. Draw five things which begin with that letter.

1

0-88012-825-9 • Traditional Manuscript

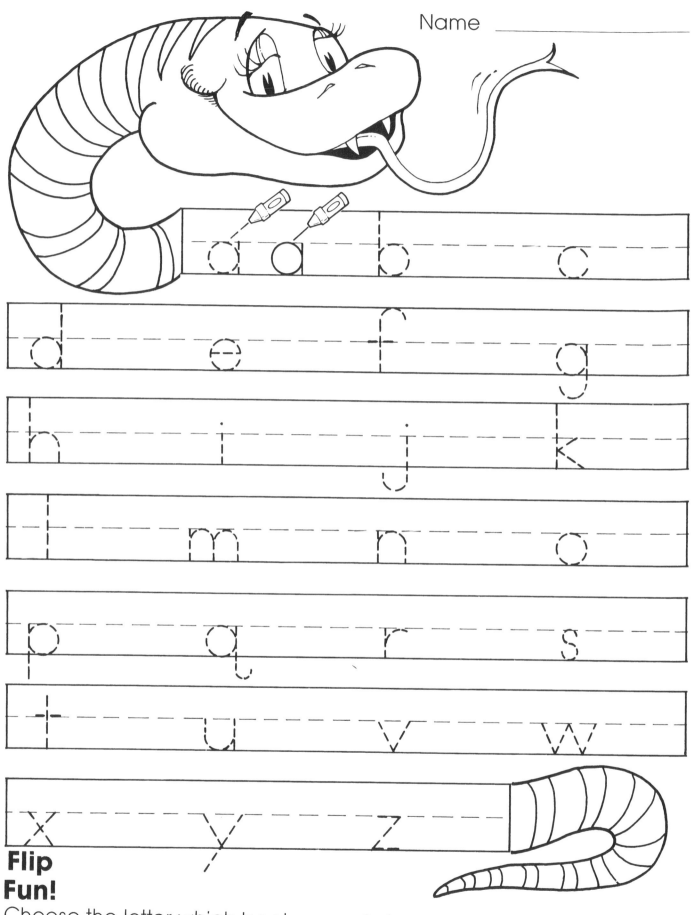

Name _____

a a b c

d e f g

h i j k

l m n o

p q r s

t u v w

x y z

Flip Fun!

Choose the letter which begins your first name. Draw five things which begin with that letter.

2   0-88012-825-9 • Traditional Manuscript

A a

A - red
a - blue

A A

a a

Anna

away

Ants are apple artists.

Flip
Fun!

Draw a tree with 3 red apples and 3 green apples.

Aa

Ants adjust accordians.

Alligators are acrobats.

Flip Fun!   Draw an alligator eating an apricot.

0-88012-825-9 • Traditional Manuscript

B b

B B B B B

b b b b b

B B

b b

B b B b

balloon

Bambi

Flip Fun!

Draw a bunny holding a red, a blue, a yellow and a green balloon.

B b

B - blue
b - orange

B   b   b   B

B B

b b

Bobby

bubbles

Baby bears bite bananas.

Flip Fun!

Draw a teddy bear eating another food that begins with B.

Bb

Bzzzzzzzzzzzz

Bzzzzzzzz

Bees buzz by bridges.

Bugs blow brass bugles.

Flip Fun! Draw a bat taking a bubble bath. Color the bubbles blue.

9

0-88012-825-9 • Traditional Manuscript

C c

CCCCC

ccccccc

Cc

c c

CcCc

castle

Cinderella

Flip Fun!

Draw five fluffy yellow clouds. Put a big blue C on each one.

C c

C - green
c - purple

C

CC

cc

Calvin

candy

Clumsy cooks carry cakes.

Flip Fun!

Draw a big yellow cake. Put blue candles on it to show how old you are.

0-88012-825-9 • Traditional Manuscript

Oo

Clowns catch candy.

Chimps cut coconuts.

Flip Fun! Draw a colorful clown.

0-88012-825-9 • Traditional Manuscript

D d

DDDDD

d d d d d

D D

d d

Dd Dd

doll

Denmark

Flip Fun!

Draw a big green dragon and two more animals that begin with D.

D d

D - orange
d - blue

d

D D

d d

David

did

Damp ducks dance.

Flip
Fun!
Draw five purple dishes. Put a brown donut on each dish.

14   0-88012-825-9 • Traditional Manuscript

D d

Ducks decorate donuts.

Dolphins direct divers.

Flip Fun! Draw a dinosaur dunking a donut.

E e

E E E E E E

e e e e e

E E

e e

E e E e

elephant

Earth

Flip Fun!

Draw eight envelopes. Put a green E on each one.

E e

E - yellow
e - purple

E

E E

e e

Ernie

every

Elves eat eight eggs.

Flip Fun!

Draw an Easter basket. Put eight colorful eggs in the basket.

5lbs.

Energetic eels exercise.

Elephants exit elevators.

Flip Fun! Draw an eel going down an escalator.

18

0-88012-825-9 • Traditional Manuscript

F f

F F F F F

f f f f f

F

f f

F f f

fish

Florida

**Flip
Fun!**

Draw five orange fish in a big black frying pan.

F f

F - red
f - brown

Name _____

F

f

F f

f f

Fred

fifth

Four fat foxes feast.

**Flip
Fun!**

Draw five things you would find on a farm.

Ff

Name _____

Five fairies fix fudge.

_____

_____

Frogs fry French fries.

_____

_____

Flip Fun!   Draw a fruit you like to eat. Color it.

21   0-88012-825-9 • Traditional Manuscript

G g

GGGGG

g g g g g

GG

g g

GgGg

ghost

Georgia

Flip
Fun!
Draw a ghost blowing a big bubble with his gum. Put a purple G on
the gum.

22

0-88012-825-9 • Traditional Manuscript

G g

G - green
g - orange

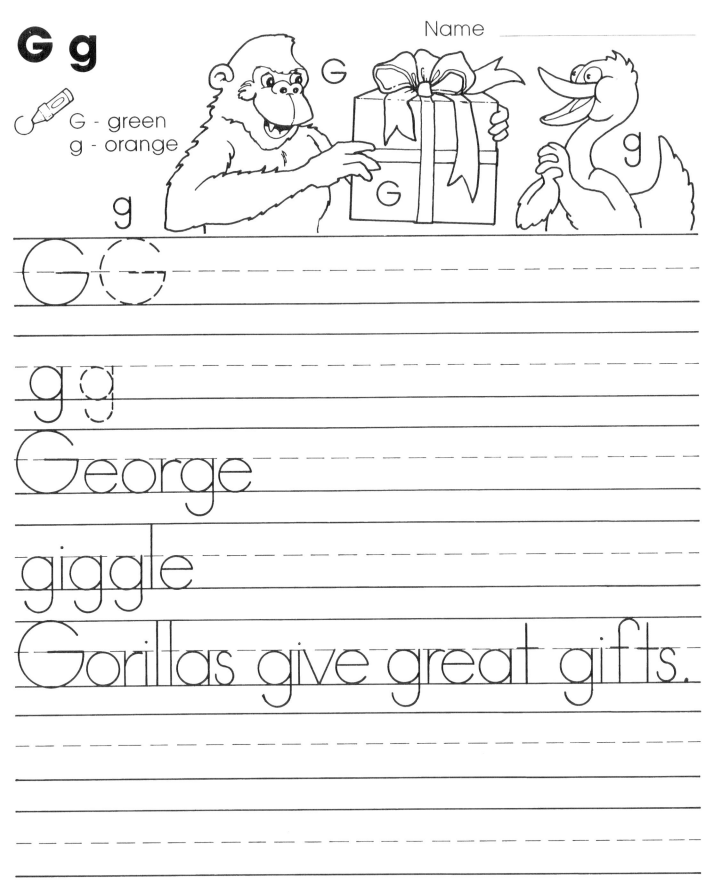

g

G G

g g

George

giggle

Gorillas give great gifts.

Flip Fun!

Draw four green gifts that begin with G.

Name _____

Grasshoppers giggle.

Geese gobble grapes.

Flip Fun! Draw a gingerbread house and a garden.

 0-88012-825-9 • Traditional Manuscript

H h

Name _____

H H H H H H

h h h h h

H

h h

H h h

hamburger

Hawaii

Flip Fun!

Draw a plate with two hamburgers and two hot dogs on it.

25
0-88012-825-9 • Traditional Manuscript

H h

H - red
h - purple

H

H H

h h

Harry

honey

Horse hotels have hay.

Flip
Fun!
Draw a big brown horse wearing a yellow hat with a red heart on it.

0-88012-825-9 • Traditional Manuscript

Hh

Hippos have huge hats.

Hogs hike high hills.

Flip Fun! Draw a helicopter.

0-88012-825-9 • Traditional Manuscript

I i

I I I I I I

i i i i i i i i

I I

i i

I I i

ice cream

India

Flip Fun!

Draw an ice cream cone with a yellow, a green, a purple and an orange scoop.

       0-88012-825-9 • Traditional Manuscript

I i

I - yellow
i - green

I

i i

Ivan

inside

Icy igloos include icicles.

Flip Fun!

Draw the inside of an igloo.

0-88012-825-9 • Traditional Manuscript

I i

Name _____

I. I.

INK

Iguanas ink initials.

Inchworms ice icicles.

Flip Fun!   Draw an island. Draw an ice-cream stand on it.

© Carson-Dellosa   30   0-88012-825-9 • Traditional Manuscript

J j

Flip Fun!

Draw three jets flying in a row. Color the first one green, the middle one orange and the last one purple.

J j

J - purple
j - green

J

J J J

j j j

John

juice

Jellybeans juggle jacks.

**Flip
Fun!**

Draw a jar filled with colorful jellybeans.

J j

Jellyfish juggle jars.

Jittery joggers jump.

Flip Fun! Draw four things you can juggle. Color each one a different color.

33

0-88012-825-9 • Traditional Manuscript

K k

K K K K K

k k k k k

K k

k k

K K K k

key

Kentucky

Flip Fun!
Draw a key ring. Put a red, a blue, a yellow, a green, a purple and an orange key on the ring.

K k

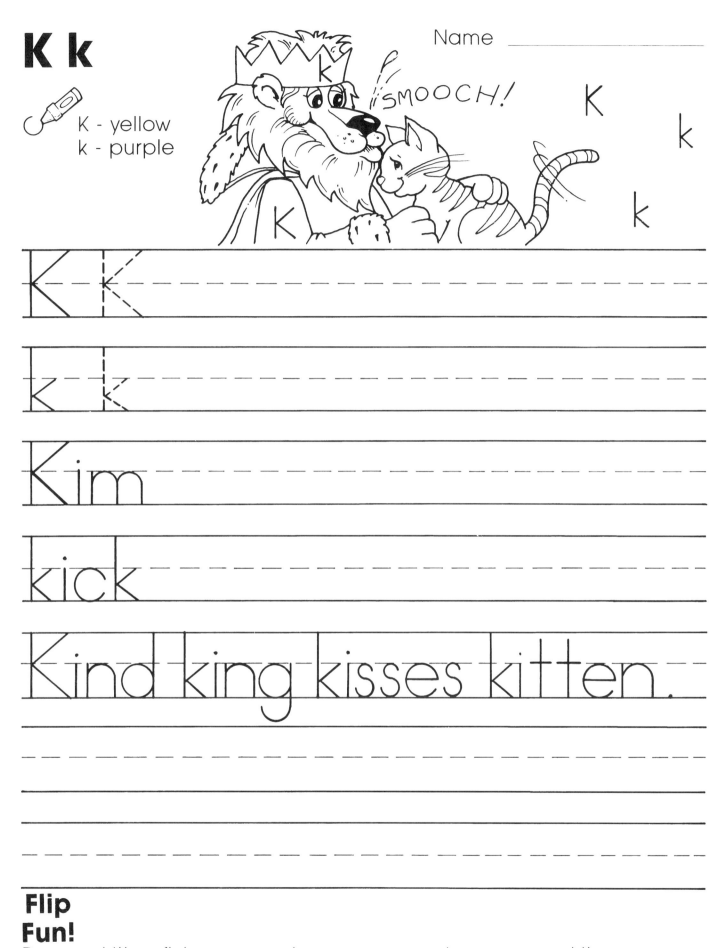

K - yellow
k - purple

Name _____

K

k

Kim

kick

Kind king kisses kitten.

**Flip
Fun!**
Draw a kitten flying a purple, a green and an orange kite.

Name _____

Koalas kindle kindness.

Kangaroos kiss kittens.

Flip Fun! Draw two knee socks. Color one red and one purple.

0-88012-825-9 • Traditional Manuscript

L l

L Lassie

L L

L

L L L

lamb

Lassie

Flip Fun!

Draw ten leaves. Color five green and five orange.

L l

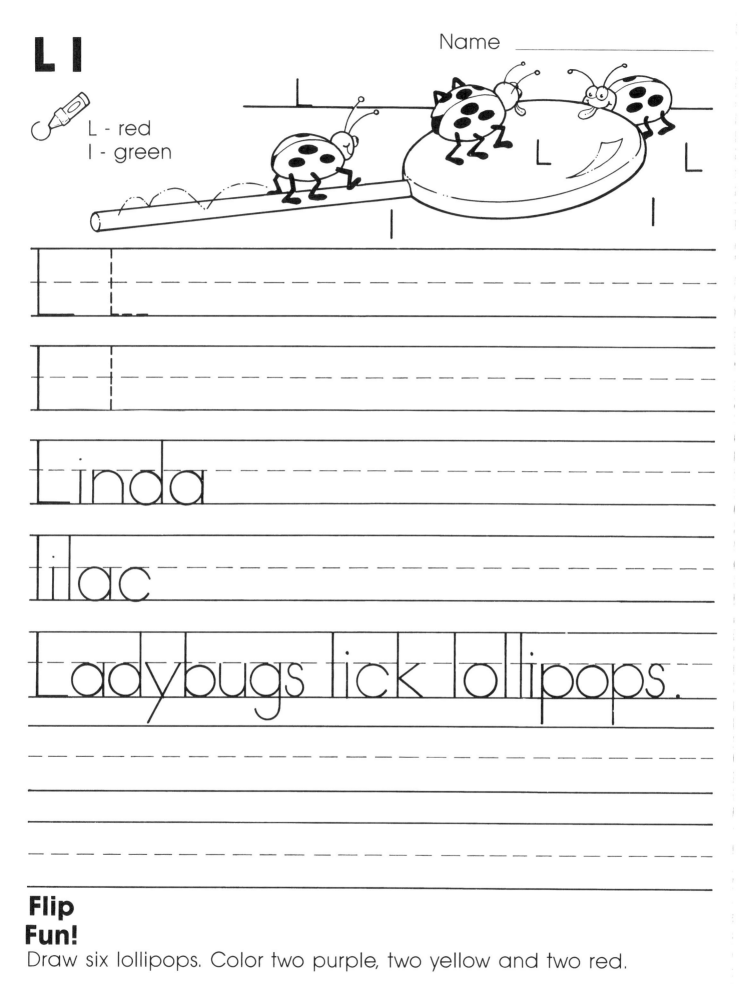

L - red
l - green

Name _____

Linda

lilac

Ladybugs lick lollipops.

**Flip
Fun!**
Draw six lollipops. Color two purple, two yellow and two red.

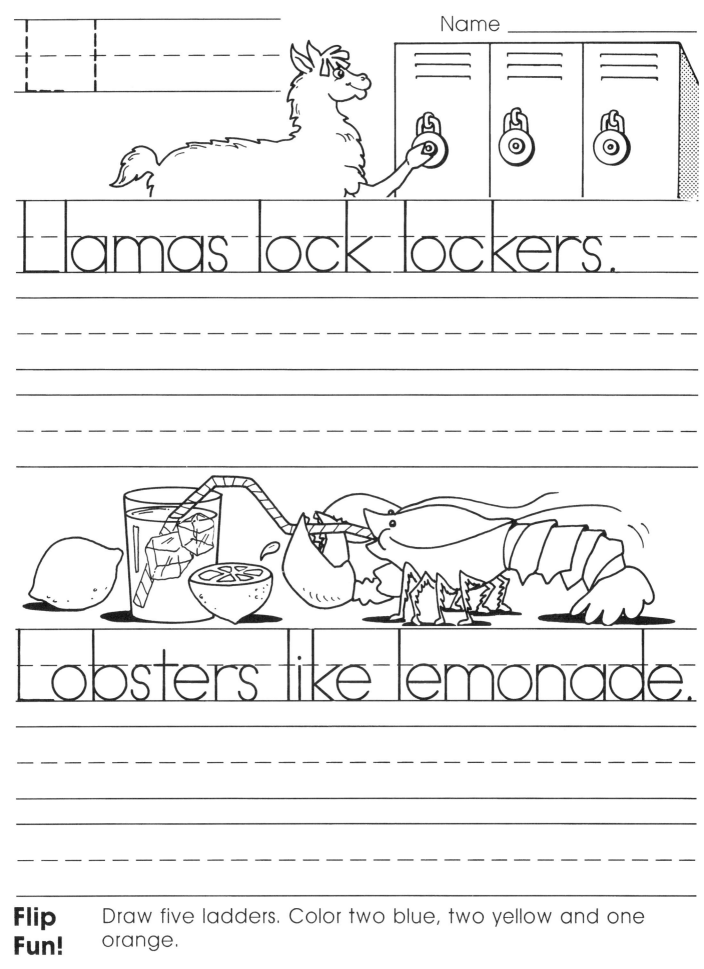

Llamas lock lockers.

Lobsters like lemonade.

Flip Fun! Draw five ladders. Color two blue, two yellow and one orange.

39 0-88012-825-9 • Traditional Manuscript

M m

MMMM

m m m m

MM

m m

MmMm

moon

Mars

Flip Fun!

Draw a picture of yourself on the moon.

M m

M - brown
m - green

M

M

m

m

MM

mm

Mary

mushroom

Mice make mud pies.

**Flip
Fun!**
Draw five brown mud pies. Put a big red M on each one.

0-88012-825-9 • Traditional Manuscript

Mm

Mary made meatballs.

Moose mix malts.

Flip Fun! Draw a mask you would like to wear. Color it.

N n

NNNNN

n n n n n

NN

n n

NnNn

nest

Neptune

Flip Fun!

Draw a brown nest with four redbirds in it. Draw a brown nest with three bluebirds in it.

 0-88012-825-9 • Traditional Manuscript

N n

N - yellow
n - purple

N

n   N   n   N

N N

n n

Nan

noon

Nurses need needles.

Flip Fun!

Draw five pictures that begin with the sound of N.

N n

Nancy needs notes.

Newts nail numbers.

Flip Fun! Draw three things you like to nibble.

O o

O O O O O

o o o o o

O O

o o

O o O o

octopus

O z

**Flip
Fun!**
Draw a picture to show an octopus living in the ocean.

0-88012-825-9 • Traditional Manuscript

O o

O - purple
o - brown

Name ____________

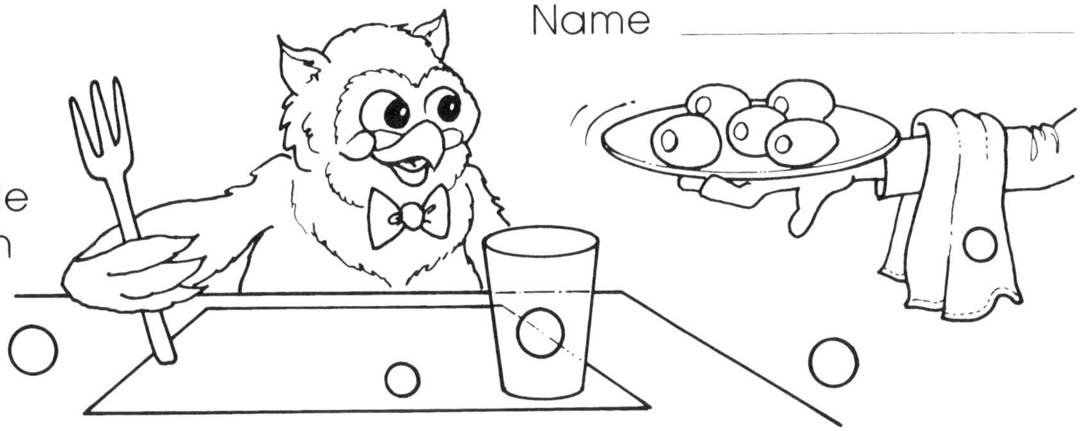

O O

o o

Oscar

ocean

Owls order oval olives.

Flip
Fun!
Draw four things with an oval shape.

0-88012-825-9 • Traditional Manuscript

Oo

Ollie opens oatmeal.

_____

_____

Oysters oil old oars.

_____

_____

Flip Fun! Draw five things that can be orange.

48

0-88012-825-9 • Traditional Manuscript

P p

P P P P P

p p p p p

P P

p p

P p P

pizza

Pluto

Flip
Fun!

Draw a big pizza divided into four pieces. Put a purple P on each piece.

P p

P - yellow
p - purple

P

P P

p p

Patty

people

Pigs plan perfect picnics.

Flip Fun!

Draw a big brown picnic basket. Draw the food you would pack for a perfect picnic.

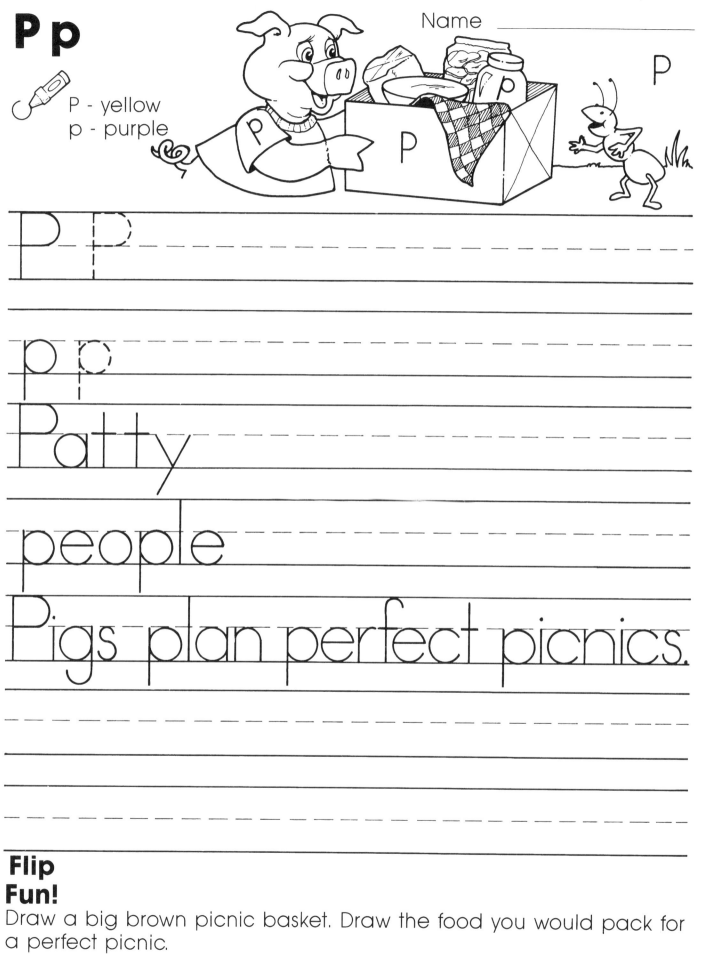

Pp

Penguins park pickups.

Pigs pop popcorn.

Flip Fun! Draw ten puffy pillows. Draw three polka dots on each one.

Q q

Q Q Q Q Q Q

q q q q q

Q Q Q

q q

Q Qq Qq

quarter

Quebec

Flip Fun!

Draw eight quarters. Draw what you would buy with eight quarters.

52 0-88012-825-9 • Traditional Manuscript

Q q

Q - red
q - green

Name _____

Q Q

q q

Quincy

quart

Queens quilt quickly.

Flip Fun!

Draw three things you do quietly.

53

0-88012-825-9 • Traditional Manuscript

Name _____

Quail quiver quietly.

Queens quilt.

Flip Fun!   Draw five things you can do quickly.

     0-88012-825-9 • Traditional Manuscript

R r

R R R R R R

r r r r r r

R R

r r

R r R r

rocket

Rome

Flip Fun!

Draw where you would like to go in space and what you would see.

55 0-88012-825-9 • Traditional Manuscript

R r

R - green
r - blue

R R

r r

Robert

river

Rabbits run races rapidly.

Flip Fun!

Draw ten fluffy rabbits' tails. Put a big red R on each one.

0-88012-825-9 • Traditional Manuscript

R r

CHEESE STEW

Rats read recipes.

50¢ 1 HOUR

FOR RENT

Robots rent rabbits.

Flip Fun! Draw a robot and you doing something together.

S s

Flip
Fun!

Draw a seal playing with six balls. Color two balls red, two balls green and two balls blue.

0-88012-825-9 • Traditional Manuscript

S s

S - orange
s - blue

S S

s s

Sarah

season

Swans sip sweet sodas.

Flip Fun!

Draw seven sodas with seven straws.

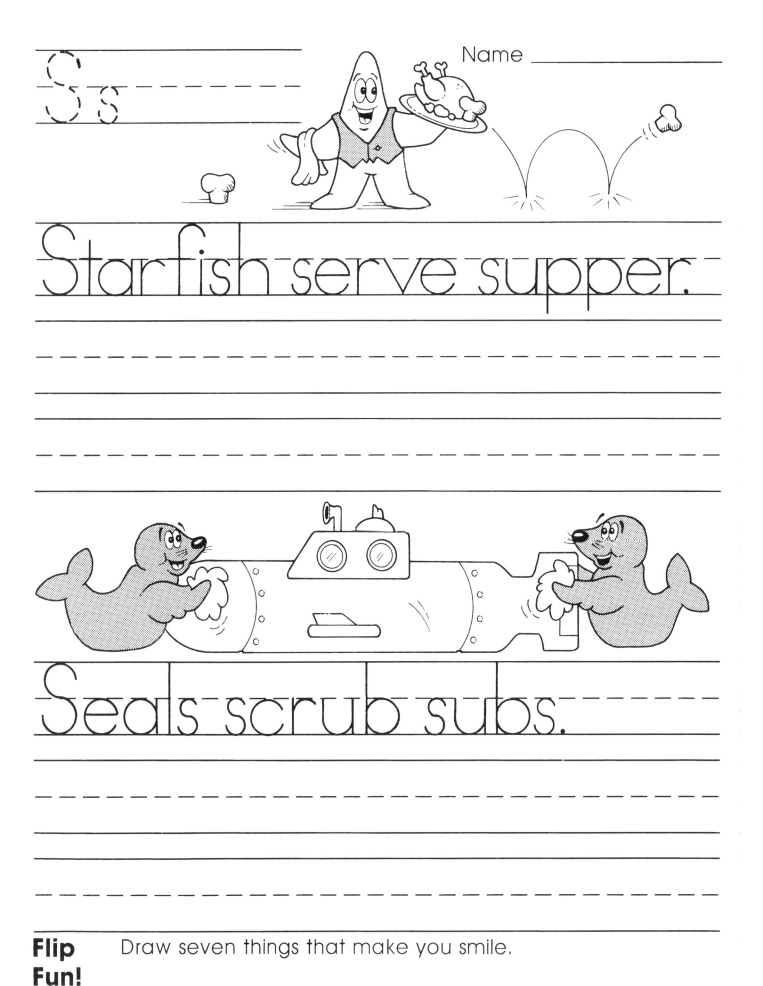

S s

Name _____

Starfish serve supper.

Seals scrub subs.

Flip Fun!   Draw seven things that make you smile.

         0-88012-825-9 • Traditional Manuscript

T t

T T T T T T

t t t t t

T T

t t

T T T T

television

Texas

Flip
Fun!
Draw a big TV. Draw your favorite program on the TV.

T t

Name

T

t

T T

t t

Tina

taste

Two toads tap-dance.

**Flip
Fun!**

Draw a turtle talking on a telephone.

Tt

Turkeys teeter-totter.

Turtles taste tacos.

Flip Fun!   Draw ten things that taste good.

0-88012-825-9 • Traditional Manuscript

U u

U U U U U

U U U U U

U U

u u

U U

umbrella

Utah

Flip
Fun!

Draw what you like to do on a rainy day.

U u

Name _____

U - purple
u - orange

U
u
U
U
u

U U

u u

Ursula

under

Unicorns use umbrellas.

Flip Fun!
Draw a place where you think unicorns might live.

U u

Umpires use umbrellas.

Unicorns undo urns.

Flip Fun! Draw four things that can be found under the sea.

V v

Name _____

V V V V V V V V V

V V V V V V V V

V V

V V

V V V

violets

Venus

Flip
Fun!

Draw a green vase filled with ten purple violets. Put a purple V on
the vase.

67   0-88012-825-9 • Traditional Manuscript

V v

Name _____

V

V

V v

Vana

vegetable

Vultures visit vampires.

Flip Fun!

Draw three things that begin with V.

Vv

Vultures view violets.

Vampires vacuum.

Flip Fun! Draw a place you would like to go on a vacation.

0-88012-825-9 • Traditional Manuscript

W w

WWWWW

w w w w w

WW

w w

WwWw

watermelon

Washington

**Flip
Fun!**
Draw a big red watermelon with ten black seeds. Draw a little red
watermelon with five black seeds.

70   0-88012-825-9 • Traditional Manuscript

W w

W - yellow
w - orange

W W

w w

Wally

window

Worms wiggle wildly.

Flip Fun!
Draw five brown worms in a swimming pool.

71 0-88012-825-9 • Traditional Manuscript

W w

Name _____

WILLY

Willy wants water.

Wasps wear wigs.

Flip Fun! Draw a picture of your favorite wig.

X x

XXXXXXXXXXX

XXXXXXXXXX

X X

X X

X X X X

x-ray

Xanadu

Flip Fun!

Draw how you might look in an x-ray.

0-88012-825-9 • Traditional Manuscript

X x

X - red
x - purple

X x X

X x

Xavier

X-ray

X-man x-rays xylophones.

Flip Fun!
Draw three more musical instruments.

Name _____

Xina x-rayed x-rays.

Xylophones Xerox x's.

Flip Fun! Draw a treasure map. Put a big X where the treasure is buried.

0-88012-825-9 • Traditional Manuscript

Y y

Y Y Y Y Y

y y y y y y

Y Y

Y Y

Y Y y

yo--yo

Yukon

Flip Fun!

Draw six yo-yos. Put a purple Y on each one.

Y y

Y - yellow
y - red

Name _____

Yolanda

yesterday

Yaks yell, "Yummy yams."

Flip Fun!

Draw a big dish of yummy, yellow yogurt.

Yy

Name _____

Yaks yank yo-yos.

Yellow yams yawn.

Flip Fun! Draw four things you do in your yard.

78

0-88012-825-9 • Traditional Manuscript

Z z

Z Z Z Z Z Z Z

Z Z Z Z Z Z

Z Z

Z Z

Z Z Z

zoo

Zeus

Flip
Fun!
Draw five zoo animals.

Z z

Z - purple
z - green

Z   Z
Z
Z
Z

Z Z

z z

Zelda

zigzag

Zebras zip zippers.

**Flip
Fun!**

Draw four things you wear that could have zippers on them.

80

0-88012-825-9 • Traditional Manuscript

Zz

Zippers zigzag.

Zany zombies zoom.

Flip Fun! Draw a design using zigzag lines. Use many different colors.

Color, trace and write.

red

blue

yellow

green

purple

orange

brown

black

Flip Fun!

Draw five pictures with your favorite color.

Trace and write.

Sunday

Monday

Tuesday

Wednesday

Thursday

Friday

Saturday

Flip Fun!

Choose your favorite day. Draw what you like to do on that day.

Color, trace and write. Name _____

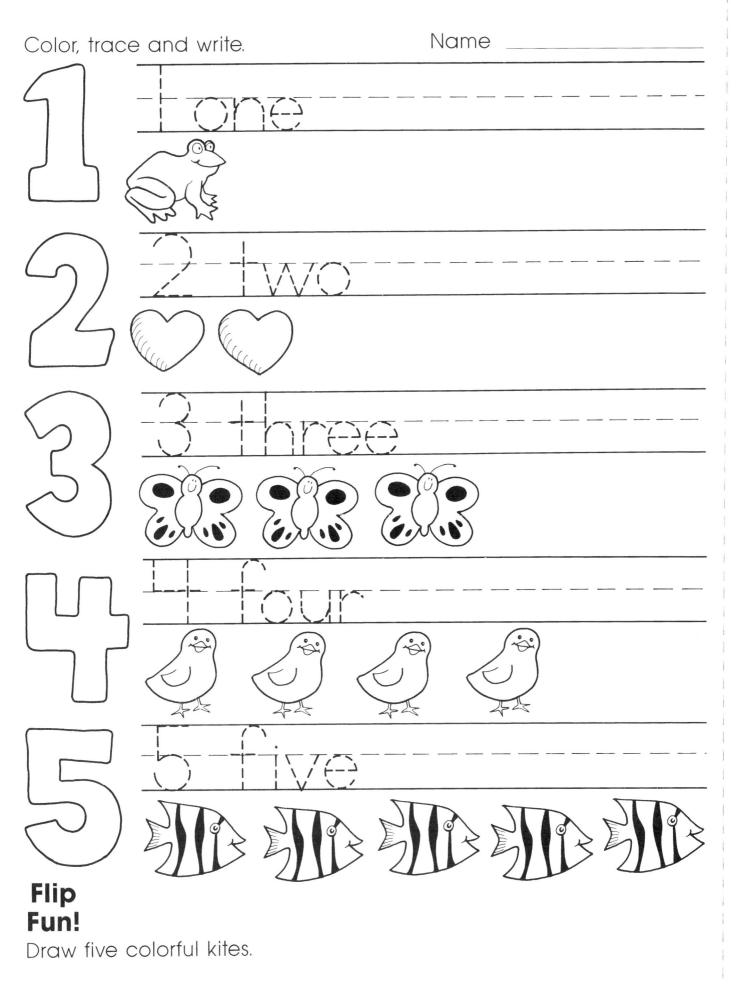

1 T one

2 2 two

3 3 three

4 4 four

5 5 five

Flip Fun!
Draw five colorful kites.

84

0-88012-825-9 • Traditional Manuscript

Color, trace and write.

Name _____

6

7

8

9

10

6 six

7 seven

8 eight

9 nine

10 ten

Flip Fun!

Draw ten colorful butterflies.

0-88012-825-9 • Traditional Manuscript

Color, trace and write.   Name _____

11 11 eleven

12 12 twelve

13 13 thirteen

14 14 fourteen

15 15 fifteen

Flip Fun! Draw fifteen colorful flowers.

                                       0-88012-825-9 • Traditional Manuscript

Color, trace and write.　　　Name _____

16　16 sixteen

17　17 seventeen

18　18 eighteen

19　19 nineteen

20　20 twenty

Flip Fun! Draw twenty colorful balloons.

　　　　　　0-88012-825-9 • Traditional Manuscript

Merry Months

Name _____

Color, trace and write.

January

February

March

April

May

June

Flip Fun! Draw a picture of what your favorite time of year looks like.

0-88012-825-9 • Traditional Manuscript

Monthly Medley

Name _____

Color, trace and write.

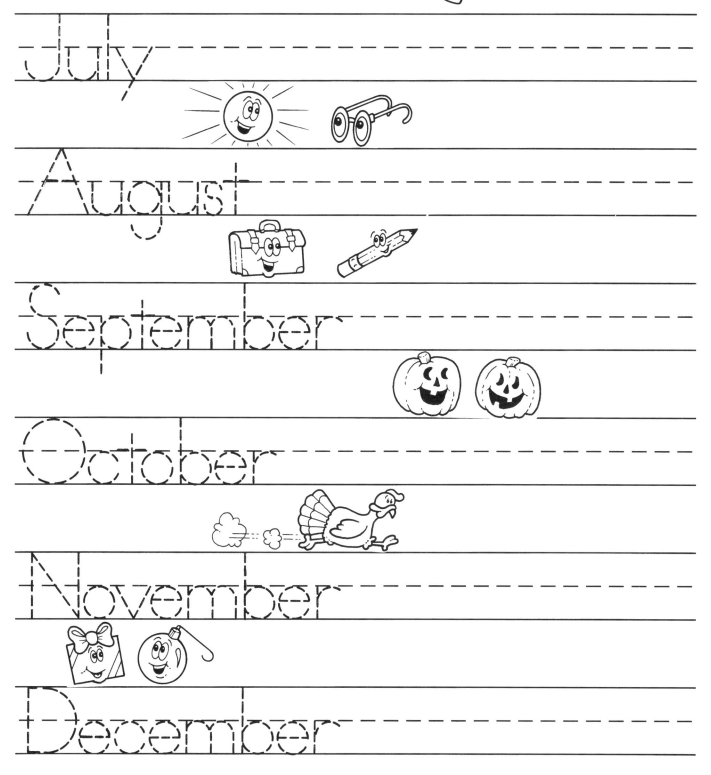

July

August

September

October

November

December

Flip Fun! Choose your favorite month. Draw a picture of what you like to do during the month.

0-88012-825-9 • Traditional Manuscript

Family Portrait

Name _____

Color, trace and write.

father _____

mother _____

sister _____

brother _____

aunt _____

uncle _____

Flip Fun! Draw a picture of your family.

Getting into Shapes

Name _____

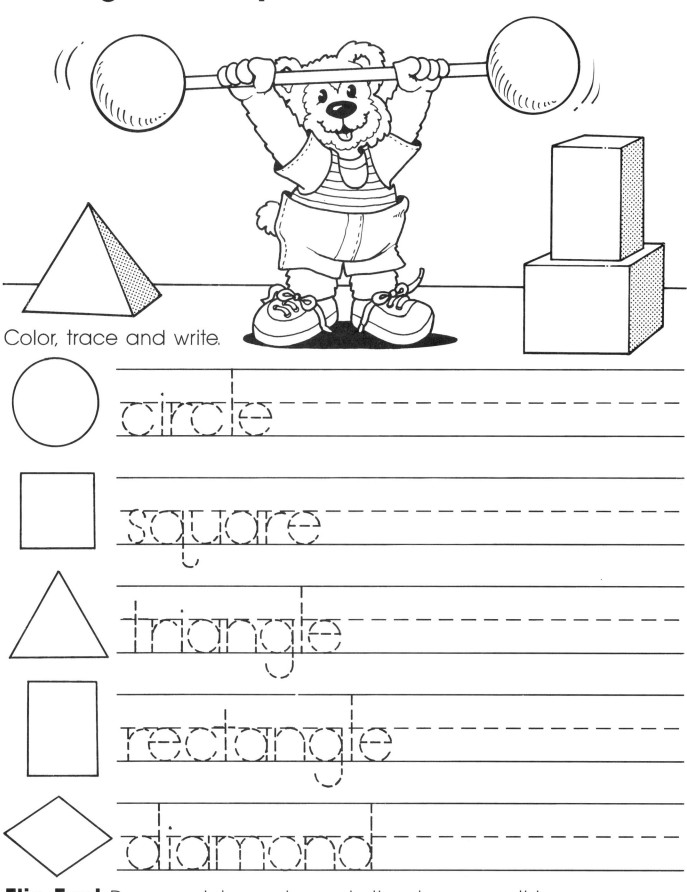

Color, trace and write.

circle

square

triangle

rectangle

diamond

Flip Fun! Draw a picture using only the shapes on this page.

0-88012-825-9 • Traditional Manuscript

Money in the Bank

Trace and write.

cents ----------------------------

penny ----------------------------

nickel ----------------------------

dime ----------------------------

quarter ----------------------------

half dollar ----------------------------

----

dollar ----------------------------

Flip Fun! Draw something you would buy with one dollar.

Where?

Name _____

Trace and write.

right

left

up

down

over

under

around

Flip Fun! Draw a cat on the left side of the paper. Draw a dog on the right.

School Is Out for the Day

Name _____

What do you like to do after school?
Trace and finish each sentence.

After School Activities

play alone	play with friends	play with pets
climb a tree	swing on a swing	read a book
jump rope	play ball	eat a snack
play soccer	watch TV	draw pictures
color pictures	play a game	paint a picture

I like to _____

I like to _____

I like to _____

I like to _____

I like to _____

I like to _____

Flip Fun! Draw a picture showing what you like to do after school.

Summer Words

sunny

fishing

sailing

swimming

hiking

dry

camping

picnic

bicycling

hot

Find the summer words in the picture. Write them on the lines.

1. _ _ _ _ _ _ _ _ _ _ _

2. _ _ _ _ _ _ _ _ _ _ _

3. _ _ _ _ _ _ _ _ _ _ _

4. _ _ _ _ _ _ _ _ _ _ _

5. _ _ _ _ _ _ _ _ _ _ _

6. _ _ _ _ _ _ _ _ _ _ _

7. _ _ _ _ _ _ _ _ _ _ _

8. _ _ _ _ _ _ _ _ _ _ _

9. _ _ _ _ _ _ _ _ _ _ _

10. _ _ _ _ _ _ _ _ _ _ _

Flip Fun! Draw what you like to do on a hot summer day.

0-88012-825-9 • Traditional Manuscript

Fairy Tale Fun

Name _____

Write the titles of five of your favorite fairy tales.

Word Bank

Beauty and the Beast	The Emperor's New Clothes
Cinderella	The Four Musicians
Goldilocks and the Three Bears	The Gingerbread Boy
Hansel and Gretel	The Little Mermaid
Sleeping Beauty	Three Billy Goats Gruff
Snow White	Three Little Pigs

1. _____

2. _____

3. _____

4. _____

5. _____

Flip Fun! Draw a picture of your favorite fairy tale.

Toys, Toys and More Toys

Name _____

Write the names of six toys you would like to have.

Word Bank

ball	baseball	basketball	bat
blocks	car	clay	computer game
crayons	doll	drum	football
jump rope	marbles	paints	puzzle
soccer ball	top	toy animal	train
bike	truck	kite	skateboard

1. _____

2. _____

3. _____

4. _____

5. _____

6. _____

Flip Fun! Draw a picture of your favorite toy.

Holidays

Name _____

Write these holidays in order starting with your favorite.

New Year's Day   Valentine's Day   Christmas

Easter   Fourth of July   Halloween

Thanksgiving

1. _____

2. _____

3. _____

4. _____

5. _____

6. _____

7. _____

Flip Fun! Draw a picture of your favorite holiday.

What a Way to Travel!

Name _____

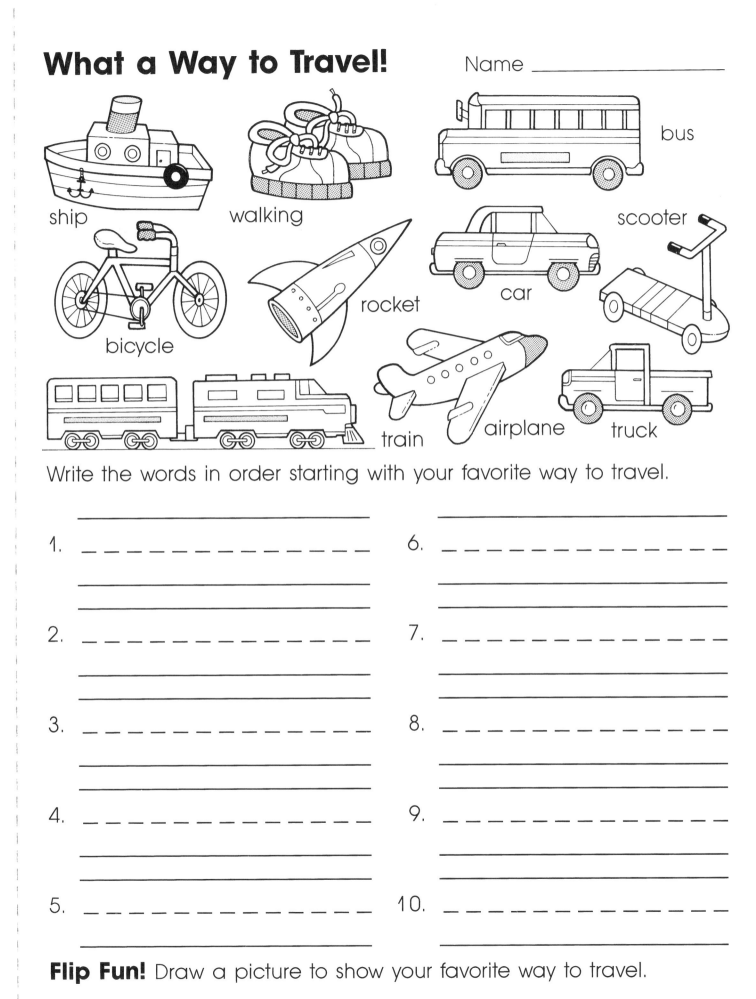

ship   walking   bus   bicycle   rocket   car   scooter   train   airplane   truck

Write the words in order starting with your favorite way to travel.

1. _____
2. _____
3. _____
4. _____
5. _____

6. _____
7. _____
8. _____
9. _____
10. _____

Flip Fun! Draw a picture to show your favorite way to travel.

Write a Rhyme

Write the titles of the nursery rhymes in alphabetical order.

Jack and Jill
Rain, Rain Go Away
Sing a Song of Sixpence
Hickory, Dickory Dock
Pease Porridge Hot
Little Bo Peep

1. _____

2. _____

3. _____

4. _____

5. _____

6. _____

Flip Fun! Draw a picture showing your favorite nursery rhyme.

What Day Did You Say?

Name _____

Copy the names of the days of the week in Spanish and in French.

Spanish	English	French
domingo		dimanche
	Sunday	
lunes		lundi
	Monday	
martes		mardi
	Tuesday	
miércoles		mercredi
	Wednesday	
jueves		jeudi
	Thursday	
viernes		vendredi
	Friday	
sábado		samedi
	Saturday	

Flip Fun! Draw what you like to do on sábado.

Ordinal Numbers

Name _____

first

second

third

fourth

fifth

sixth

seventh

Write the correct word to tell where each runner placed in the race.

1. _____

2. _____

3. _____

4. _____

5. _____

6. _____

7. _____

Flip Fun! Draw a prize you would like to receive for winning a race.

Far Out!

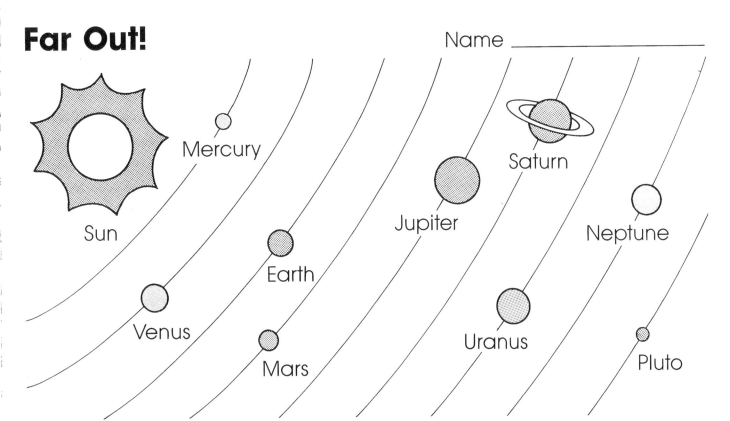

Imagine that you are traveling from the sun to outer space. Write Sun first. Then write the names of the planets in order starting with Mercury.

1. _ _ _ _ _ _ _ _ _ _ _ _ _   6. _ _ _ _ _ _ _ _ _ _ _ _ _

2. _ _ _ _ _ _ _ _ _ _ _ _ _   7. _ _ _ _ _ _ _ _ _ _ _ _ _

3. _ _ _ _ _ _ _ _ _ _ _ _ _   8. _ _ _ _ _ _ _ _ _ _ _ _ _

4. _ _ _ _ _ _ _ _ _ _ _ _ _   9. _ _ _ _ _ _ _ _ _ _ _ _ _

5. _ _ _ _ _ _ _ _ _ _ _ _ _   10. _ _ _ _ _ _ _ _ _ _ _ _ _

Flip Fun! Draw what you think life could be like on another planet.

Attack of the Sweet Tooth

Name _____

Write the "sweet treats" in alphabetical order.

Word Bank				
pie	doughnut	ice cream	cookie	brownie
milk shake	cupcake	sundae	fudge	cake

1. _ _ _ _ _ _ _ _ _ _ _ _ _

2. _ _ _ _ _ _ _ _ _ _ _ _ _

3. _ _ _ _ _ _ _ _ _ _ _ _ _

4. _ _ _ _ _ _ _ _ _ _ _ _ _

5. _ _ _ _ _ _ _ _ _ _ _ _ _

6. _ _ _ _ _ _ _ _ _ _ _ _ _

7. _ _ _ _ _ _ _ _ _ _ _ _ _

8. _ _ _ _ _ _ _ _ _ _ _ _ _

9. _ _ _ _ _ _ _ _ _ _ _ _ _

10. _ _ _ _ _ _ _ _ _ _ _ _ _

Flip Fun! Draw your favorite "sweet treat."

Countries Around the World

Write the names of these countries in alphabetical order.

Spain	Germany	Canada	Japan	Australia
Norway	Mexico	United States	France	China

1. _____

2. _____

3. _____

4. _____

5. _____

6. _____

7. _____

8. _____

9. _____

10. _____

Flip Fun! Draw a picture of where you would like to go.

     0-88012-825-9 • Traditional Manuscript

Add It Up!

Name _____

Add. Write the answer. Then write the number word for the answer.

1	2	3	4	5
one	two	three	four	five

```
  0                        2
+ 4      _____       + 3      _____

         - - - - -                - - - - -

         _____                _____


  2                        1
+ 2      _____       + 2      _____

         - - - - -                - - - - -

         _____                _____


  1                        1
+ 1      _____       + 4      _____

         - - - - -                - - - - -

         _____                _____


  1                        3
+ 0      _____       + 1      _____

         - - - - -                - - - - -

         _____                _____
```

Flip Fun! Write five addition problems. Write the answers to the problems.

     0-88012-825-9 • Traditional Manuscript

Add It One More Time!

Add. Write the answer. Then write the number word for the answer.

6	7	8	9	10
six	seven	eight	nine	ten

$$\begin{array}{r} 5 \\ +5 \\ \hline \end{array}$$
_____
_ _ _ _ _ _ _ _ _ _

$$\begin{array}{r} 3 \\ +4 \\ \hline \end{array}$$
_____
_ _ _ _ _ _ _ _ _ _

$$\begin{array}{r} 4 \\ +2 \\ \hline \end{array}$$
_____
_ _ _ _ _ _ _ _ _ _

$$\begin{array}{r} 8 \\ +1 \\ \hline \end{array}$$
_____
_ _ _ _ _ _ _ _ _ _

$$\begin{array}{r} 3 \\ +5 \\ \hline \end{array}$$
_____
_ _ _ _ _ _ _ _ _ _

$$\begin{array}{r} 6 \\ +4 \\ \hline \end{array}$$
_____
_ _ _ _ _ _ _ _ _ _

$$\begin{array}{r} 1 \\ +6 \\ \hline \end{array}$$
_____
_ _ _ _ _ _ _ _ _ _

$$\begin{array}{r} 4 \\ +4 \\ \hline \end{array}$$
_____
_ _ _ _ _ _ _ _ _ _

Flip Fun! Write five addition problems. Have a friend solve them.

Take It Away!

Subtract. Write the answer. Then write the number word for the answer.

1	2	3	4	5
one	two	three	four	five

$$\begin{array}{r} 5 \\ -2 \\ \hline \end{array}$$ _____

$$\begin{array}{r} 4 \\ -3 \\ \hline \end{array}$$ _____

$$\begin{array}{r} 4 \\ -2 \\ \hline \end{array}$$ _____

$$\begin{array}{r} 5 \\ -0 \\ \hline \end{array}$$ _____

$$\begin{array}{r} 5 \\ -1 \\ \hline \end{array}$$ _____

$$\begin{array}{r} 4 \\ -1 \\ \hline \end{array}$$ _____

$$\begin{array}{r} 5 \\ -3 \\ \hline \end{array}$$ _____

$$\begin{array}{r} 5 \\ -4 \\ \hline \end{array}$$ _____

Flip Fun! Write five different subtraction problems.

Take Some More Away!

Name _____

Subtract. Write the answer. Then write the number word for the answer.

6	7	8	9	10
six	seven	eight	nine	ten

```
  10
-  2
_____   _____
- - - -   - - - - - -
_____   _____
```

```
   9
-  3
_____   _____
- - - -   - - - - - -
_____   _____
```

```
   8
-  1
_____   _____
- - - -   - - - - - -
_____   _____
```

```
  10
-  0
_____   _____
- - - -   - - - - - -
_____   _____
```

```
  10
-  1
_____   _____
- - - -   - - - - - -
_____   _____
```

```
   8
-  2
_____   _____
- - - -   - - - - - -
_____   _____
```

```
   9
-  2
_____   _____
- - - -   - - - - - -
_____   _____
```

```
  10
-  4
_____   _____
- - - -   - - - - - -
_____   _____
```

Flip Fun! Show 8 – 5 apples.

109
0-88012-825-9 • Traditional Manuscript

Antonym Search

Find the word in the Word Bank to match each picture. Then, draw a line to the word that means the opposite.

Word Bank

cold	down	fat	outside
hot	happy	over	inside
sad	thin	under	up

hot

Flip Fun! Draw a picture of something hard and something soft.

0-88012-825-9 • Traditional Manuscript

Get It Together

Name _____

Write two words that name things that go together. Write the word **and** between the two words.

Word Bank					
bacon	cake	cheese	cookies	crackers	eggs
ice cream	salt	key	lock	milk	pepper
		socks	shoes		

1. bacon and eggs

2. _____

3. _____

4. _____

5. _____

6. _____

7. _____

Flip Fun! Draw a picture of two things that go together.

Connect the Compounds

Name _____

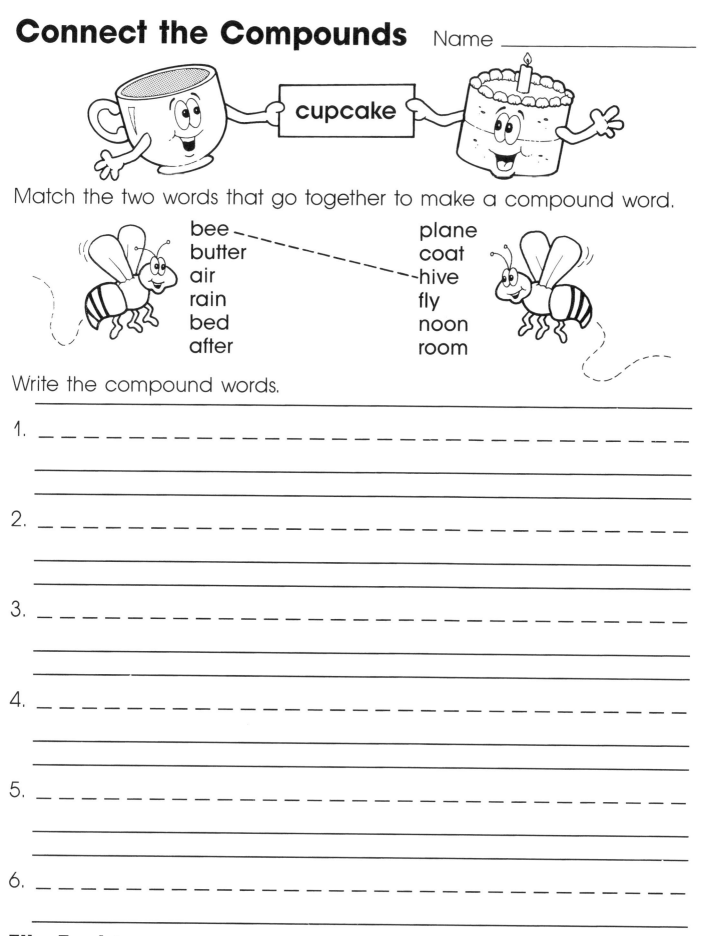

cupcake

Match the two words that go together to make a compound word.

bee	plane
butter	coat
air	hive
rain	fly
bed	noon
after	room

Write the compound words.

1. _____

2. _____

3. _____

4. _____

5. _____

6. _____

Flip Fun! Draw a beehive and five bees.

 0-88012-825-9 • Traditional Manuscript

It Just Makes Sense

Name _____

touching	hearing	tasting	seeing	smelling

Read the words. Write which sense you would use to find out if something is…

1. loud _____

2. sweet _____

3. burning _____

4. yellow _____

5. cold _____

6. salty _____

7. soft _____

8. ringing _____

Flip Fun! Draw a picture showing something you like to see.

 0-88012-825-9 • Traditional Manuscript

We're Off and Shopping

Name _____

Write the words from the Word Bank below the store where the items would be found.

Word Bank

birdcage	bread	cat	dog	drum
flour	hamster	horn	meat	milk
piano	records	sugar	trumpet	turtle

Grocery Store

_____

Pet Store

_____

Music Store

_____

Flip Fun! Draw a picture of a pet you would like to have.

0-88012-825-9 • Traditional Manuscript

All About School

Name _____

Write each of the school words under the correct heading.

Word Bank

crayons	scissors	pencils	boys	girls	glue
handwriting	books	secretary	librarian	math	science
paper	health	social studies	principal	reading	teachers

Classroom Things	Subjects	People

Flip Fun! Draw a picture of your school.

Nouns and Verbs

Name _____

Nouns are words that **name** people, places or things. Verbs are **action** words. Write the words where they belong.

Word Bank			
bite	children	donkey	house
jump	kitten	hop	run
school	skip	lunchbox	write

Nouns	Verbs

Flip Fun! Draw a picture of one of the nouns.

Which Direction Should I Go?

North

Name _____

West

South

East

Look at the map. Write the missing direction words in the blanks. Then, copy the sentences on the lines.

1. The tree is in the _____.

_____

_____

_____

2. There is a swing in the _____ and _____.

_____

_____

_____

3. The gate is to the _____.

_____

_____

_____

Flip Fun! Draw you and your friend playing in a park.

 0-88012-825-9 • Traditional Manuscript

A Magical Magic Trick

Name _____

Unscramble each sentence. Write them correctly on the lines.

1. _____

_____

2. _____

_____

3. _____

_____

Flip Fun! Draw a magic trick that you would like to be able to do.

     0-88012-825-9 • Traditional Manuscript

Barrel Full of Laughs

Name _____

1 is a clown. Goofy

2 juggles ten He oranges.

3 inside He rolls barrels.

4 claps. Everyone

Unscramble the sentences. Write them correctly on the lines.

1. _____

_____

_____

2. _____

_____

_____

3. _____

_____

_____

4. _____

_____

Flip Fun! Draw a clown doing a silly trick.

Trail Tracks

Name _____

Follow the animal tracks to the basket. Write the words in order to make sentences.

1. _____

_____

_____

_____

2. _____

_____

_____

_____

3. _____

_____

_____

_____

Flip Fun! Draw a big rabbit with a carrot.

0-88012-825-9 • Traditional Manuscript

Put It Together

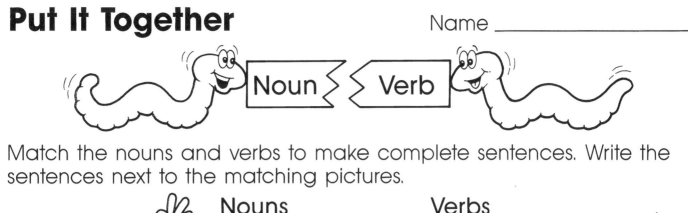

Match the nouns and verbs to make complete sentences. Write the sentences next to the matching pictures.

Nouns	Verbs
A balloon	falls.
The car	pops.
Three bells	speeds.
One apple	eats.
An ape	bakes.
My mom	ring.

1. _____

2. _____

3. _____

4. _____

5. _____

6. _____

Flip Fun! Write a sentence of your own. Draw a picture to go with it.

What's Cooking?

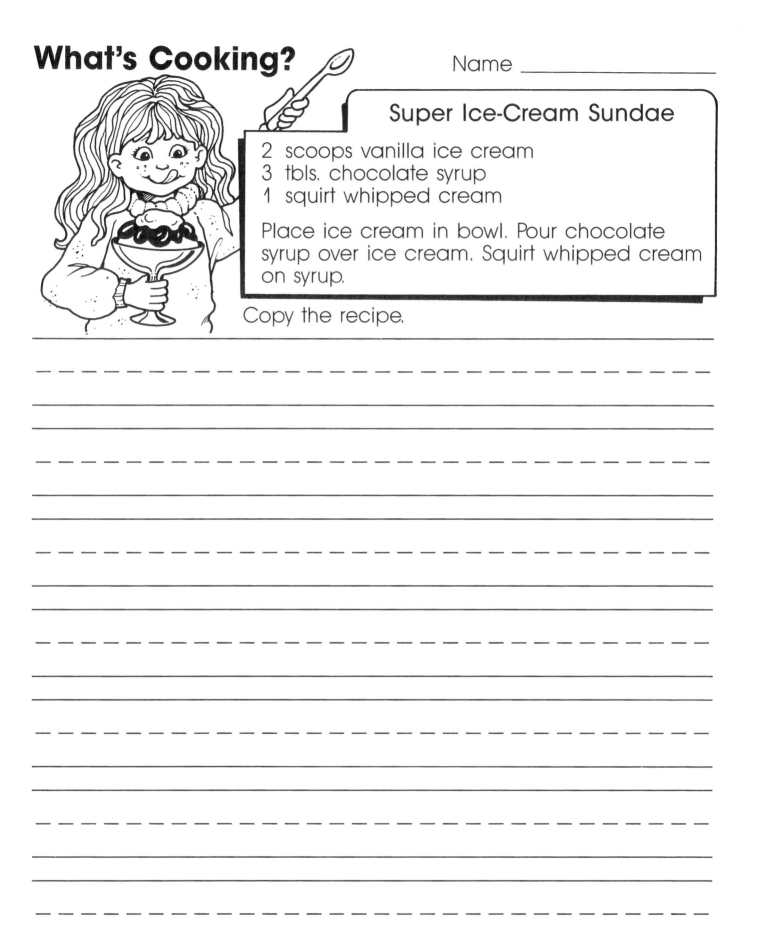

Super Ice-Cream Sundae

2 scoops vanilla ice cream
3 tbls. chocolate syrup
1 squirt whipped cream

Place ice cream in bowl. Pour chocolate syrup over ice cream. Squirt whipped cream on syrup.

Copy the recipe.

Flip Fun! Draw a yummy ice-cream sundae.

Week Days

Name _____

Write the sentences correctly with capital letters and question marks where they belong.

Sun.	Mon.	Tues.	Wed.	Thurs.	Fri.	Sat.
picnic	school	movie	museum	park	play	zoo

is sunday or monday the first day of the week

do you watch cartoons on saturday

are we going to see the movie on tuesday or wednesday

Flip Fun! Draw what you like to do on Saturday.

0-88012-825-9 • Traditional Manuscript

Months

Name _____

Write the sentences correctly with capital letters and question marks where they belong.

will it snow in december

_____

_____

_____

how hot does it get in july and august

_____

_____

_____

does school start in september

_____

_____

_____

does your family eat a big feast in november

_____

_____

_____

Flip Fun! Draw a picture of a snow fort you might build.

More Months!

Write the sentences correctly with capital
letters and periods where they belong.

kevin and i like to build snow forts in january

summer vacation begins in june

we give cards to our friends in february

i found a four-leaf clover last march

Flip Fun! Draw a beautiful flower garden.

Write Your Own

Name _____

The bunny hopped home.

Write your own sentences. Combine words from each list to make complete sentences. Write the sentences on the lines.

List 1	List 2	List 3
Two cars	dropped	the big box.
A tiny bunny	raced	around the track.
They	hopped	high.
He	runs	the ball.
The kitten	swing	into the basket.
We	kicks	after the string.

1. _____

_____

2. _____

_____

3. _____

_____

4. _____

_____

5. _____

_____

6. _____

_____

Flip Fun! Draw a picture of one of the sentences you wrote.

 0-88012-825-9 • Traditional Manuscript

Feelings

Copy and finish each sentence.

When I feel happy, I...

_____

- -

_____

When I feel sad, I...

_____

- -

_____

When I feel silly, I...

_____

- -

_____

When I feel angry, I...

_____

- -

_____

When I feel scared, I...

_____

- -

_____

When I feel excited, I...

_____

- -

_____

Flip Fun! Draw a picture of you doing something silly.

Color and write.

My name

_____

My school

_____

My street

_____

My phone

_____

My city

_____

My state

_____

0-88012-825-9 • Traditional Manuscript